DECORATIVE
TOLE
PAINTING

by B. Kay Fraser

Crown Publishers, Inc. / New York

Greeting cards used with permission of
Norcross, Inc., copyright: "Contemporary
Love Bird" (page 83) and "Happy Hippo" (page 86).

Mixed fruit pattern (page 60 and in color section)
courtesy of Craft Course Publishers, Inc.,
Rosemead, California, from their book
"Decorative Painting: Tole & Dutch & Plain Jean."

Poppy pattern (page 42 and in color section) and
"God Bless This House" design (page 90 and in
color section) courtesy of Marguerite Weaver
from her book "Paintin' Patterns."

Library of Congress Catalog Card Number: 70-185072
ISBN: 0-517-501309
ISBN: 0-517-503735
Printed in the United States of America
Published simultaneously in Canada by General
Publishing Company Limited
Designed by Margery Kronengold
Second Printing, January, 1973

Contents

Chapter 1

Tole Painting — The Folk Art That's Even More Fun Today!

If you yearn for a decorative art that's inexpensive and requires little talent yet is absolutely beautiful, then start tole painting.

Tole painting is inexpensive because it can be applied to anything made of wood or metal—from battered breadboards to rusty milk cans. It requires little talent because only one basic brush stroke must be mastered, and patterns tell you exactly where to put that stroke. With these simple ingredients, however, you can paint colorful designs that will cheer your home, impress friends, and make thoughtful gifts.

That's why tole painting is fast becoming the most popular hobby of today's creative Americans. Here's how it all began. From the middle of the 18th century to the time of the Civil War, early American settlers brightened their homes and livened up dreary winters by applying painted designs to their household goods. Historians call these designs "folk art"; they were simple patterns or stencils painted by just plain folks.

Each colony or settlement developed their own favorite designs and techniques. The French in New York, for example, developed the most sophisticated patterns—elaborate flower arrangements, exquisite birds, stylized hearts, and intricate scrolling. In fact, the American dollar still uses the scrolling originated by the French. French settlers made the most lasting contribution to the art, however, with their word "tole," which means tin.

While the French were busy painting fancy designs on tinware, the Germans in Pennsylvania were developing their own particular brand of folk art. In crude earth colors, the Germans painted flat two-dimensional figures with symbolic meaning. Their "tree of life" design, for instance, represents the continuity of birth, death, and regeneration. Their peacock is painted looking backward at its tail—a sign of renewal, since the tail is lost and regrown every year. In addition, the Germans painted hex signs on their barns to ward off evil spirits.

Also in Pennsylvania, Dutch settlers developed designs that reflected their everyday life: family members, fruit, flowers, and birds. A special favorite of the Dutch was their beloved tulip—a fond reminder of the "old country."

Scandinavians, too, perfected in paint a cherished flower from the old country, the rose. Because their roses are so lovely and unique, the art is often called by its original name, "rosemahling" (*mahling* means painting). In addition, Scandinavians perked up folk art with brighter colors and more realistic-looking patterns.

No matter what the early settlers' original nationality, they all symbolized their allegiance to American democracy with designs of guns, powder horns, and the cherished eagle, which is the most widely recreated pattern today.

But tole painting became a lost art with the Civil War and the coming of industrialization. It might have remained a lost art, too, if collecting antiques hadn't become popular. Collectors of antiques began searching for these original tole-painted wares, and found it was nearly impossible to locate relics in good condition. As settlers *used* their tole-painted items, serving trays became blistered with hot coffee spills. Deed boxes, silent butlers, chests, and chairs became scuffed.

Thus, in order to restore tole-painted relics to their original condition, antiques collectors started tole painting. And it turned out to be incredibly easy because all designs—of all nationalities—were based on one simple brush stroke.

What's more, tole painting was not only easy but fun. Soon the new crop of tole painters had decorated all their antiques and looked to new items to paint: unfinished furniture, decorative wooden plaques, bread boxes, and canisters. In the process, new techniques were developed, designs of different settlers were combined, and many new patterns were created.

Today the popularity of tole painting has blossomed to the point where nearly every town in America boasts a tole-painting instructor. Many cabinet-makers have given up all other business just to provide wares for tole painters. Accomplished painters are lining their pockets with profits from selling their tolework. Books and magazines are catering to the art.

And, just to really prove tole's popularity, it is already an item of controversy. Although "tole" has become the commonly accepted name of today's folk art, some painters believe the term is not appropriate unless we actually paint yesteryear's rustic designs on tin. Another dispute centers around the term "decorative art." Many painters think we should leave the names "tole" and "folk art" to our forefathers because modern art supplies and realistic contemporary designs make this a decorative art. Let's compromise and call it "decorative tole painting." After all, the methods used today are much more sophisticated than those of our ancestors. But it is still a folk art—techniques are easy enough for all us "folks."

Whatever you call it, decorative tole painting means fun, relaxation, and beauty. So, let's get started!

Chapter 2

First, Brush Strokes
and Practice

Tole-painted designs look so professional and so creative that it's hard to believe all designs are based on patterns and one basic brush stroke. Patterns are so simple that they resemble the plain black lines in a child's coloring book. The brush stroke itself is only a huge comma.

How can you, too, turn patterns and brush strokes into a tole-painted work of art? There are two answers: good-quality supplies and practice. You can practice later, but first you'll need to dash to the art or hobby store for supplies. The initial investment in tole-painting supplies will cost between $10 and $20—a small price for unlimited hours of fun!

A workable arrangement of tole-painting supplies.

Tole Painting Supplies

Here's what you'll need.

Artist's Oils. In theory, three colors—red, blue, and yellow—can be mixed to create any color of the rainbow. But most beginning tole painters prefer to buy their oils already mixed in tubes. Popular colors that will enable you to paint all the patterns given in later chapters are:

alizarin crimson	prussian blue
vermilion red	burnt sienna
cadmium orange	yellow ochre, light
cadmium yellow, medium	burnt umber
lemon yellow	raw umber
yellow green	payne's gray
permanent green, light	titanium white
viridian green	

White and burnt umber should be purchased in large tubes because you will use white constantly—both as a solid color and as a lightener with other colors. Burnt umber will be used for most of your antiquing.

Other colors should be purchased in small tubes until favorite color selections are made. For example, you may find that lemon yellow is too bright to suit you and later substitute chrome yellow in its place. Or, you may decide to paint grapes with magenta instead of prussian blue. If you develop a preference for transparent leaves, you can discard permanent green for sap green. Also, colors vary from brand to brand. Vermilion red in one brand may create realistic apples; but in another brand, the color may be too orange. So, experiment with the colors given in small tubes and later buy large tubes in colors you frequently use.

Select quality oils. Inexpensive paints can be lumpy, oily, and may crack with age. Always cap your tubes immediately after putting paint on the palette, for oils will dry out. And, finally, when you have a tube whose cap refuses to budge, don't force it open. Simply hold a match under the cap, and let the flame loosen it for you.

Flow Medium. Because artist's oils are thick and dry slowly, varnish is mixed with the oil to accelerate drying and to thin the flow of paint. Use a nonplastic satin-finish varnish obtainable at hardware or paint stores. (Varnishes containing plastic may cause artist's oil to bubble.)

Since varnish dries rapidly when exposed to air, buy a small can rather than a large can, which may become "gunky" with use. When painting, it's a good idea to spoon varnish out of the can into an old jar lid. Then seal the can tightly and use varnish as needed from the lid. Thus, the remaining varnish will have minimum exposure to air. Some tole painters even store their varnish in the refrigerator to slow the drying process!

Turpentine is also used in the painting process to keep the brush clean, soft, and maneuverable. Some turpentines will turn yellow with age, so play it safe by picking up gum spirits turpentine; it costs a little less at hardware stores than in the art store. It is economical to buy large quantities of turpentine, then pour a small amount in a baby food jar for use while painting.

Palette and Knife. A palette will be needed to mix artist's oils with varnish. Wooden palettes are dandy, but paper palettes don't require cleaning and may be thrown away when finished. Paper palettes may also be stored in the freezer overnight if a painting is not completed. However, some tole painters simply substitute wax paper for paper palettes.

Palette knives are available with either straight or crooked handles.

Either will work to mix your oils and scrape unwanted oil off the palette. One art supplier has observed that men generally prefer straight handles and women most often choose a crooked handle.

Brushes. Watercolor brushes are used in tole painting because the soft bristles create excellent brush strokes. Select sable brushes of the finest quality you can afford, for poor brushes make poor brush strokes.

Three brushes are all that are needed: the "brush" brush, a "liner" brush, and a "wipe-out" brush. The "brush" brush, either a #5 or #6 round-tipped brush, is the most important. (A #6 makes a larger stroke.) Whenever "brush" is referred to, this is the brush meant, for you will use it constantly. With it, you can easily create flowers, leaves, some fruit, and all basic strokes.

The "liner" is a #2 round-tipped brush used occasionally for stems, lines, dots, itty-bitty flower petals, and squiggles. You may substitute a smaller #1 brush for your liner if you prefer tinier lines.

The "wipe-out" brush is a #5 flat-tipped brush that may be used to create some fruit or flat-edged flower petals. However, the wipe-out brush is most often used to wipe out (naturally!) mistakes. By first dipping this brush in turpentine, you can wipe out paint that goes outside pattern lines or change the shape of a basic stroke that isn't quite right. In other words, you can use the wipe-out brush as you would an eraser.

Although you may later wish to add to your brush collection, these three brushes will last through years and years of painting with proper care. Proper care is easy: simply wash them in turpentine when you're done, then rinse them in soap and water to make sure that all excess paint is removed. Store with bristles up. If the shape of the brush loses its roundness, apply vaseline and reshape.

Tracing and Graphite Paper. You will not need these supplies until you actually select your first pattern. But you must buy them at art or hobby stores, so you might as well pick them up while you're there.

Tracing paper is used to copy patterns and is available in pads or rolls—either will do. Graphite paper comes in large sheets and a variety of colors. Buy a dark sheet to use when painting patterns on a light background and a light sheet to use for dark backgrounds. These graphite sheets are sandwiched between the tracing paper and the object you are tole painting to transfer the design. Do not substitute carbon paper, for it will smear and be difficult to remove.

Clean-up Supplies. Some tole painters are messy. Their artist's oils stain clothing and tabletops. Others manage to emerge from a tole-painting session fresh as the daisies they have painted. If you suspect that you may be the messy type, protect your clothing with an artist's smock or old shirt. Table-tops are easily protected by laying old newspaper under your materials.

Even if you're the neat type, you will need to clean paint off your brush and hands occasionally. Keep a box of facial tissues or paper towels handy for this purpose (much easier than using rags).

How to Mix the Medium

With ingredients assembled, let's begin the fun of mixing oils.

Earlier it was pointed out that varnish is used with the artist's oil to create a "flow medium." Now that sounds terribly professional, but simply it amounts to this: squeeze a half inch of oil in your favorite color on the palette. Add an equal proportion of varnish to the oil and mash them together with the palette knife until the mixture has a whipped-cream consistency. (Poke with the tip of the palette knife to see if it will form peaks like whipped cream.) Then dip the brush in turpentine, wipe lightly on a tissue, and load the brush with the oil-varnish mixture. That's all there is to it.

The correct oil-varnish mixture will peak like whipped cream.

Applying paint to your brush is called "loading" because the brush is not poked or jabbed into the paint as is often done in other arts. Rather, the brush is loaded by laying it sideways, then patting and rolling in the edge of the paint mound until bristles are coated with color.

When the brush is loaded, you can test the paint for the right consistency by making strokes on the palette paper. If the paint flows easily off the brush, no problem. If, however, the paint clings to the brush, add more varnish; if the paint drips onto the paper, add more artist's oil.

Generally, equal proportions of varnish and oil will give you the correct consistency. But because varnishes vary in thickness from brand to brand, you may have to add more varnish or more oil to reach the whipped-cream consistency. Also, if you are painting over a long period of time or in a very warm room, the paint mixture will begin to dry. No problem! Just add more varnish until the oil is once again at the correct consistency.

Although this consistency is used most often, there will be times when you prefer a thinner mixture. The thinner the mixture, the more transparent it will be. So, if you desire leaves with a "see-through" effect, mix more varnish into the oil. A thinner mixture is also more workable when using the liner brush to create stems, squiggles, or lettering.

As a guideline, remember that the whipped-cream consistency will give you texture—the lovely highs and lows of basic stroke flower petals, bird feathers, flower centers, clothing, ribbons, fruit, etc. But, if you do not desire a textured appearance, then you may paint with a thinner consistency.

The Basic Brush Stroke

This is it! It's finally time to try your hand at the strokes that separate tole painting from other arts. Decorative tole painting is composed of tiny—almost fussy—brush strokes that take a few hours to perfect. Do not be discouraged if your first strokes look like tracks of a chicken with flat feet. Folk art has survived hundreds of years because early Americans took time to create beautiful brush strokes. With patience and practice you can too. Here's how.

Dip the brush in turpentine, wipe, then load with paint. Hold the brush low and tight on the ferrule (the metal part). Control over the brush is crucial and best achieved by holding the brush with thumb, index, and middle finger. Using the palette paper or tracing paper for practice, press your hand on the paper, steadying your hand with the little finger. An elbow raised up and out from the shoulder will aid in the swinging motion necessary to make brush strokes.

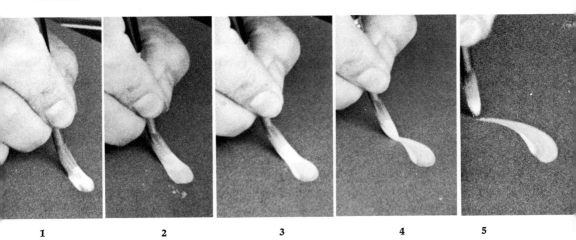

1 2 3 4 5

(1) Begin the stroke by pressing down on the brush. Use your little finger as an anchor. (2) Slowly pull the brush toward you as you gradually decrease pressure by lifting up on the brush. (3) Swing the brush ever so slightly to the right, still decreasing pressure. (4) By lifting and swinging the brush, you will create a tapered tail on the stroke. (5) Actual size of completed stroke.

Practice, practice, practice this basic stroke until you can at least begin to duplicate the stroke illustrated. (Remember to reload the brush after every few strokes!) Try swinging your brush to the left—or don't swing it at all. Apply long heavy pressure or short light pressure. See how the shape of your stroke depends entirely on how hard you press and when you release the pressure.

To learn more about varying the pressure and to make practice more fun, copy the basic stroke designs illustrated. Simply place your tracing paper over the designs and fill them in with the basic stroke; if you're really brave, try it freehand. You'll recognize many of the designs here because they're used on today's paper cups and candy tins and were used yesteryear on country tinware. In fact, if you are lucky enough to own an original piece of folk art, you can restore it with these brush strokes.

If, after continued practice, you still are not satisfied with the basic stroke, it may be that you are not holding the brush correctly; the paint may be too thick or too thin; you may be rolling your brush rather than lifting up

Popular basic stroke designs.

to get the point. Perhaps the brush has become too full of paint and should be wiped clean with paper towels or tissue.

Check these things out, but don't give up! The basic stroke is really the *only* thing you need to learn, so stick with it. Although some beginning tole painters have spent ten hours practicing before perfecting the stroke, you should create a bona fide basic stroke in one or two hours. And when you see that little tail taper just the way you want it to, all your practice will have been worthwhile!

Blend Colors for Realism

Today's decorative tole painters strive for realism. Fruit looks so juicy and natural that you could sink your teeth into it. Bouquets appear to be fresh plucked from the yard. And, if anybody tole-paints poison oak, you'll probably start itching!

Two techniques give realism—texture and shading. Because you have mastered the basic stroke, you are already using texture. Note how your bristles spread to create high and low ridges on the basic stroke. In other words, your strokes were not blobbed in with flat solid color. Rather, the combination of whipped-cream paint and pressure and release motions created strokes of varying texture. In fact, you can feel the highs and lows of brush strokes with your finger (but wait until the paint dries!). This texture makes flower petals and bird feathers as true to life as nature's own.

But it's not enough. For the utmost in natural beauty, you should also copy Mother Nature's shading. For example, if you look at a daisy in the sun, you'll see that the daisy may look brighter in some spots, darker in others, depending on where the sun strikes it. You can create the same natural shades by color blending.

Color blending is simply a different method of loading paint onto your brush. First, you must decide what the basic color is; then the highlight color; then the shade color. For example, the leaf is one basic color—say, permanent green. But it appears to have a highlight where the sun shines—maybe yellow green. And, where no sun shines, the leaf looks much darker—like viridian green. So, when painting a leaf, load the brush with the basic color, then dip lightly in the highlight color before making the stroke. Make the stroke and you'll create a beautifully highlighted leaf. Then load the brush in the basic color and dip in the shade color. Presto, a nicely shaded leaf.

Sound complicated? It's not. Color blending is actually easy and fun. Let's try it (and learn how to paint leaves in the process)! Beginning with one-stroke leaves, color-blend these leaf designs in permanent green, using yellow green for a highlight. Then try shading the basic color with viridian green instead of highlighting.

Two-stroke leaves are equally easy. Make one stroke of permanent green dipped in yellow green. Right next to it, make another stroke of permanent green dipped in viridian green. This gives you both highlight and shading.

Another way to create two-stroke leaves is to make one stroke in permanent green. Next to it place a stroke in yellow green. Then pull the brush through the middle of the strokes to blend the colors. A tiny basic stroke of yellow green may be placed on the tip of the leaf.

Finally, multistroke leaves should be considered. As you can see, large leaves are simply basic stroke upon basic stroke. But they are very impressive when color-blended. Some artists color-blend each stroke exactly· as if they

Two-stroke leaves.

One-stroke leaves.

Multistroke leaves.

were one-stroke leaves. However, large leaves have more realism when the tip is highlighted and the base is shaded. Start at the base of the leaf, painting your way down one side at a time. The base of the leaf may be shaded with viridian green—toward the middle use almost pure permanent green—and gradually pick up more highlight until the tip shows almost pure yellow green.

Another large leaf idea is to shade one side of the leaf and highlight the other side. This technique makes the leaf appear to "turn," as leaves often do in a breeze.

Often two-stroke and multistroke leaves will overlap each other. Use more shading on the underneath leaves and more highlight on the top leaves. This makes the dark leaves appear farther away and the lighter leaves seem closer to you.

Now, thumb ahead to the pattern chapters and see if your color-blended leaves resemble those of experienced tole painters. Chances are they do, for color blending is a very easy yet beautiful way to imitate nature.

Because we are imitating nature when color blending, there are no set rules about which colors to blend. In fact, some tole artists don't use green at all to paint leaves. Instead, they blend yellow and burnt umber, yellow and prussian blue, or yellow and raw umber to create natural-looking leaves. It will be easiest at first to use greens, of course. But, after some experience, if you wish to try blending other colors, simply pluck a leaf from your yard and use it as a guide.

Chapter 3

Next, Get the
Whole Picture

Now you're ready to try honest-to-goodness decorative tole painting. No more practice! But perhaps a few questions will arise, such as: What should I tole paint? How should I prepare it? What background color should I use? Does the object need to be antiqued? How do I put the pattern on the object? Are there any little tole tricks?

The answers to all these questions are simple. Yet the answers are very important. So let's get the whole picture by considering each question before you actually start tole painting.

What May Be Tole Painted

Collecting items to tole paint is nearly as much fun as tole painting itself. Any item of tin or wood may be painted. Because your first painting will be somewhat of an experiment, you will be wise to paint something inexpensive and replaceable. Suggested wooden items are decorative plaques, breadboards, door panels, bowls, spoons, recipe boxes, and cheese boards. Tinware could be coffeepots, pitchers, lard buckets, bread boxes, serving trays, canisters, watering cans, or cookie tins.

Many tole painters develop strong preferences for certain objects. For example, some specialize in painting decorative wooden plaques. Plaques may be purchased in hobby stores, variety stores, or even obtained through mail-order catalogs. Any plaque used for decoupage work may also be used for tole. The *Sears Craft Fun Catalog*, for instance, contains many decoupage plaques and boxes that would be lovely tole painted (write Sears, Roebuck and Co., 2465 Utah Avenue, Dept. 139KC, Seattle, Washington 98134, for a free copy).

A less expensive idea for plaques, however, is to visit a lumberyard and ask for scrap wood. If you want a plain-edged square or rectangle, ask them to cut a fir board (at least ½-inch thick) in your chosen size. Or, a trip to the beach will provide free driftwood that makes a novel background for tole designs. And don't overlook razed barns and homes in your neighborhood, for old wood makes elegant plaques.

Still other tole painters pooh-pooh decorative plaques and demand useful objects. They browse secondhand stores, garage sales, and dime stores for tin and wooden objects that serve a practical purpose. These painters turn milk cans into umbrella holders and barstools; old mailboxes into bread boxes; and cigar boxes into jewelry cases. If you, too, are of a practical mind, consider tole-painting cutting boards, picnic baskets, laundry hampers, kitchen-utensil holders, key-chain decorations, tabletops, chairs, dressers, pet dishes—even toilet seats!

Raggedy Ann scarecrow on plaque
by Charlene Messerle.

Eagle on milk can
by Billie Middleton.

Dogwood flowers on serving tray
by Sylvia Sauter.

Mixed fruit on cutting paddle
by B. Kay Fraser.

Happy hippo on plaque
by B. Kay Fraser.

Mushrooms on canister
by Jerry Berg.

Apples on antique bread-warming pan
by Billie Middleton.

Little girl on plaque
by B. Kay Fraser.

Federal eagle on plaque
by Jerry Berg.

Sunflowers on coal bucket
by Sylvia Sauter.

*Mixed fruit on coffee table
by Billie Middleton.*

*Apples on rocker
by Billie Middleton.*

*Strawberries on bedstead
by Sue Simmoneau.*

*Apples on pepper grinder
by Jerry Berg.*

*Child's face on milk stool
by Francie Richardson.*

*Mixed fruit on milk can
by Sylvia Sauter.*

*Wedding invitation on plaque
by Jerry Berg.*

*Fanciful animal plaques
by Chris Messerle.*

*Scroll and dogwood flowers on board
by Sylvia Sauter.*

*Lemons on silverware chest
by Sue Simmoneau.*

*Mouse on mousetrap
by Carolyn Nordahl.*

*Strawberries and daisies on metal sewing basket
by Sylvia Sauter.*

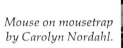

Corn on French bread paddle
by Charlene Messerle.

French heart on tabletop
by Joyce Pinnock.

Poppies on board
by Sylvia Sauter.

There's another group of tole artists who definitely prefer to paint antiques, since these were the objects originally used for folk art. Their work is extremely impressive on pepper grinders, coal buckets, spittoons, tobacco boxes, deed boxes, butter paddles, camelback trunks, kitchen hutches, and old rocking chairs. A word of caution: antiques are most valuable when preserved in their original condition. So, it is recommended that you do not tole paint a valued antique unless the object needs restoring or would be definitely improved by a tole-painted design.

Surely your mind is buzzing with things you can tole paint by now. Browse the following chapters to see how many of these objects look with a tole-painted design.

How to Prepare an Object

No matter what you select to tole paint, it must have a smooth surface for two reasons. First, brush strokes are difficult to create on bumpy, irregular surfaces. Second, folk art at its finest boasts a rich, hand-rubbed finish that is only possible on smooth surfaces.

New wooden objects may already be smooth. Feel them. Chances are there will be no irregularities on cutting paddles and cheese boards. Plaques may only require a light sanding. But older wooden items can require more effort, for often the old finish must be removed. Varnish and paint may be taken off with commercial paint removers or coarse sandpaper. Shellac may be removed with rubbing alcohol.

Then the wood must be sanded smooth, following the grain of the wood as you sand. Remember that wormholes, dents, and distressing marks do not have to be sanded out if you desire an antique effect. When a wooden object finally feels smooth to the touch, seal the finish with a wood sealer, available at the hardware store.

Tin objects are prepared a bit differently from wood to prevent rusting. When rust has already started, sand it off or use a wire brush. Whether new or old, wash the tinware in soap and hot water; rinse with water; then rinse with vinegar to neutralize metal acids.

Tin also requires a protective coat of rust-retardant metal paint, also at the hardware store. A favorite color is off-white because a large can will last a long time and can be easily covered no matter what color you select for a base coat.

Applying the Base Coat

Both tin and wooden objects are ready for the next step—applying the base coat. The base coat is the background color for the design and it covers the entire object.

Before deciding which color you prefer, again get the whole picture. What background color would blend well with the colors you plan to use in the tole-painted design? Where will the painting be placed when completed—will it match that room's decor? Is the tole design fanciful and gay and thus appropriate for a bright colored background? Or is it delicate and subdued—ideal for a muted shade?

The most popular background colors among today's tole artists are rich reds, olive greens, dull golds, cheerful yellows, Dutch blues, stark white, and natural wood. In addition, many painters antique the object, either before or after applying the design, for a silky, shaded effect. If you, too, desire to antique the object, select a bright background color—for antiquing will tone it down.

Use any brand of good-quality satin-finish enamel for your base coat. Satin finishes are recommended because gloss finishes can be slippery, making your strokes more difficult to control. Or, if a natural wood background is desired, use the same satin-finish varnish that you mix with artist's oil. Be sure to stir the paint and varnish well to mix in the desired coloration and finish. (The finish may be glossy instead of satin if you don't stir well!) Also, never shake the varnish can to stir, for that will cause bubbles.

When you apply the base coat, follow the grain with wooden objects. Tinware such as pots, buckets, and cans should be painted going around the object, not up and down. Round trays, on the other hand, will have conflicting lines if painted around and should be painted straight, as you would a board—although the rim may be painted around.

One base coat may be sufficient since you have already sealed the wood or applied a coat of rust-retardant paint to tin. However, most tole painters prefer at least two and sometimes three coats of the background color. Additional coats give a smoother, richer appearance.

To ensure that additional coats adhere to the item, lightly sand with steel wool or fine-grain sandpaper between coats. This delicate sanding also removes grit and imperfections (such as bubbles!) that may occur while painting. Again, follow the grain of wood while sanding. Sanding residue may easily be removed by wiping the object with a rag dipped in turpentine or with a tack rag.

Now, if preparing the object and applying the base coat sounds like a chore, that's because it is a chore! You'll soon discover that tole painting is so much fun that it's worth the effort; but in the meantime, here are a few short-cuts. To end the agony of paint-brush cleanup between coats, try painting with small squares of foam rubber (available in sheets at variety stores, foam rubber may be discarded after use). Instead of cleaning the brush used for varnish, wrap it in tinfoil and stick it in the freezer. You'll use varnish later on to protect your tole design, so select a good quality brush and never use it for anything except varnish. Stir paints and varnish with old swizzle sticks or chopsticks that you were going to throw away anyway. It is possible to save time by using spray paints; however, spray paints are more expensive and sometimes blob and drip.

How to Antique

Antiquing gives the rich, warm, aged look to tole painting. Indeed, antiquing is the crowning touch and may take as much time as painting the design. Basically, antiquing is a three-step process: (1) applying the antiquing glaze; (2) brushing for shading; and (3) wiping for highlights. The remaining glaze will duplicate the hand-rubbed look of original early American tole art.

Although the antiquing glaze is most often applied *after* the tole painting is finished, it may be applied *before* you tole paint if a special effect is desired. For example, if you desire a rustic-looking object but prefer to shade the design as you tole paint, then you would antique *before* tole painting. If you would rather shade and highlight the tole design with antiquing glaze, then you would antique *after* tole painting. Or, if you want an extra rich, silky appearance, you may antique both before and after!

Occasionally you may not antique at all. If you are painting an old board that already has natural shading and highlights, antiquing won't be necessary. Or, you may transform a new wooden plaque into an "old" one by burning with a blowtorch. Another time when you may decide not to antique is when the tole design is very fanciful—perhaps owls painted on driftwood or impressionistic animals on a child's plaque.

But, remember, we're getting the whole picture before tole painting, so you must now decide when or if you are going to antique. If you are not, continue on to the pattern instructions. If you choose to antique *after* tole painting, return to this page when your design is completed and has been given two coats of varnish (to protect the artist's oil during antiquing). If, however, you choose to antique *before* tole painting, let's get started!

To antique, you will need (of course!) an antiquing glaze. This may be purchased ready-mixed in hobby and hardware stores. Frankly, if you mix your own glaze, you will have a wider choice of colors; the glaze consistency will be superior; and it will be much, much cheaper. The glaze recipe is simple: it consists of equal parts of turpentine and artist's oil. You will also need a good-quality, soft-bristled paintbrush for shading, or use a shaving brush. Rub the antiquing brush on your cheek—if it feels soft, it's a dandy! A soft cloth or tissue will be required during the last step of antiquing—highlighting. Lintless rags, nylon stockings, silk scarves, or facial tissues may be used. Keep in mind that the texture of the cloth or paper will give a similar texture to the glaze. For example, silk scarves will create a lovely, silky texture.

With ingredients assembled, you're ready to begin antiquing. Mixing the glaze comes first. As noted, equal proportions of turpentine and artist's oil should give the desired hand-lotion consistency. Mix small quantities in an old saucer, and larger amounts in a baby food jar. The glaze should drain slowly down the side of the jar, coating the glass. Or, if the mixture will shake gently from the brush, it is also correct.

What color artist's oil should you use? Burnt umber is by far the most popular because it gives the look of shaded, hand-rubbed walnut. Burnt sienna is sometimes chosen for its "maple" effect. However, any color may be used as long as it is darker than the base coat. And it's fun to experiment! For example, a pink base-coat antiqued in alizarin crimson and a dab of payne's gray is breathtaking. A light blue base coat antiqued in permanent green gives a turquoise effect. And, a dark brown base coat antiqued in payne's gray offers the ultimate in a rustic, aged look.

Okay, the color has been chosen and the glaze is mixed. You're ready for step one: applying the glaze. Using any handy paintbrush, cover the entire item with glaze. (On large objects, cover only a portion at a time, such as a chair seat or one dresser drawer.) Don't panic—the antiquing glaze will completely hide the tole-painted design. Let the glaze dry until it loses its gloss—from five to twenty minutes or more, depending upon the warmth of the room.

When the shine dims, you can begin step two—brushing for shading. Work the glaze back and forth, up and down. The soft, dry bristles will work the glaze into nooks and crannies as well as remove excess glaze. Wipe the brush clean with paper towels or tissue every few swipes. Because you are striving for a shaded, aged look, be sure to leave plenty of glaze in places that would be naturally shaded with age such as curves, crevices, edges, corners, etc. Keep brushing until the tole design emerges. Or, if the design hasn't yet been applied, keep brushing until the glaze is as dark or light as you desire. (Only you can decide this!)

The final step is to highlight by wiping. Softly rub the cloth or tissue in tiny circular motions in places where more highlight is desired. Again, be guided by what would naturally be lighter if the object were an antique. Handles, drawer pulls, flat surfaces, and arm rests, for example, would all

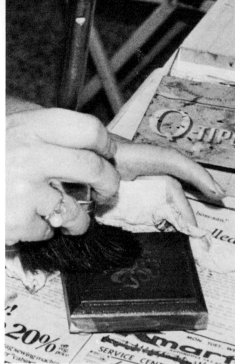

Cover the entire object with glaze.

Shade with a soft-bristled brush.

be lighter with wear. You may also decide to draw attention to the tole design by highlighting the area around it—or vice versa; shade the design and highlight the rest of the object.

You may also give the tole painting additional highlights by wiping glaze off the design with cotton swabs or toothpicks wrapped in cotton.

Continue wiping, removing excess glaze from the cloth on newspapers (or find a clean patch of cloth). It may be easier to hold the cloth if it is wadded up into a ball. Blend the highlighted areas into the shaded areas so

Antiquing is the crowning touch to tole painting. Painting by Joyce Pinnock.

Rub glaze with cloth or tissue for highlights.

there is a gradual change from dark to light rather than a distinct break. Work carefully, and don't become impatient; your reward will be a beautifully shaded work of art that looks satiny smooth and professional!

Unfortunately, every tole painter has an antiquing failure now and then. This usually happens when the glaze becomes too dry to "work," or if the glaze mixture is either too thick or too thin. Failures are easily remedied: just wipe the glaze off with turpentine and start over. The two coats of varnish applied over the tole design will protect it from the turpentine.

When you are satisfied with your antiquing, put the object in a safe place to dry—safe from lint, safe from little fingers that love to touch things. If you antiqued *before* tole painting, you will now need to apply two coats of satin-finish varnish over the antiquing. This will protect the glaze throughout the painting process.

If you antiqued *after* tole painting, two coats of well-stirred satin-finish varnish should be sufficient to protect both the glaze and the design. No need to sand between coats because sanding may remove the base color and artist's oil. Additional varnish will further enhance the "must touch" look of tolework. Although plastic varnish should never be used directly on tole paint or antiquing, you may use plastic varnish if you first apply two coats of regular varnish for protection. In fact, if the object will be subject to heavy use—as would be a serving tray, stool, chair, or such—it is recommended that you do give it the additional protection of plastic varnish.

Pick a Pattern

The big moment has finally arrived! It's time to browse the following chapters for the pattern of your choice. Beginners will find daisies and Queen Anne's lace are both very, very lovely and very, very easy.

Once the pattern is selected, it must be transferred to the object you want to tole paint. Here's where the tracing paper and graphite paper are used. Place the tracing paper over the pattern and copy. Then place the traced design exactly where you want it to be on the object. Prevent slippage by fastening the tracing paper pattern with masking tape. Next sandwich the graphite paper, sticky side down, between the object and design. Use dark graphite paper on light backgrounds, and light graphite paper on dark backgrounds. Trace lightly with a pencil or the end of your liner brush, and the pattern will be transferred and ready to paint!

Tracing paper and graphite paper are used to transfer the pattern to your object.

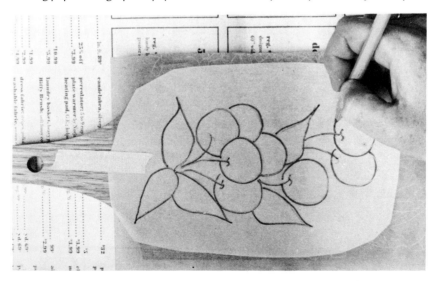

Tracing is simple, of course. But do keep two things in mind. First, trace with soft pressure. Heavy lines may be difficult to cover with artist's oil and may score the wood. Secondly, trace only the main features of the design. Dots, squiggles, small flowers, etc., are easily added freehand, so don't waste your time copying them. You may keep your pattern in front of you as you paint if you have any questions about where a dot or squiggle should be. Also, pattern lines that aren't covered can be removed with a cotton swab dunked in turpentine after the tole painting has dried.

Although tole painting is a folk art because patterns keep things simple enough for everybody, many people prefer to change patterns—just a little bit! For example, you may desire a design larger or smaller than the one shown. If so, simply draw squares around the original design. Then, draw smaller or larger squares to scale and fill in with the design, as shown.

Enlarge or reduce any design with squares drawn to scale.

Another common way to change patterns is to combine designs. You may wish a strawberry from one pattern, a daisy from another, and a heart from still another design. Again the tracing paper will come in handy. Just trace what you wish from each design; cut out and "play" with the designs until they form a pleasing arrangement. Then trace this arrangement, and you'll have your very own original new pattern.

Although an excellent selection of decorative tole patterns is presented in this book, you will want to expand your pattern collection. Actually, patterns are as easy to find as items to tole paint. Simply use tracing paper and pencil to copy patterns from magazines, calendars, crewel and embroidery designs, needlepoint patterns, children's books, greeting cards, advertisements, labels—or even walk into an antique or gift shop and ask to copy other painters' tole patterns! If money is no object, you may buy patterns in art stores; but with so many free patterns available, it is not a necessary expenditure.

Undercoating and Sponging

By now, you certainly have the whole tole-painting picture. But you may be wondering if there aren't some little "tricks" that tole painters use. Yes! These tricks are called undercoating and sponging. When painting flowers and leaves, these techniques are not normally used. However, when you reach the fruit patterns, you'll want to know all about these tricks.

Undercoating is simply giving a pattern an extra coat of paint for added depth. For example, if you are painting people, fruit, vegetables, or clothes, you may wish these objects to stand out more than background leaves and flowers. So give them an extra coat of paint.

The undercoat may be thinner than the usual whipped-cream consistency, and generally is a mixture of white and yellow or ochre. An undercoat of stark white may be difficult to cover with the final coat. The undercoat may be applied with a brush or with a tiny sponge.

When using a brush, apply the paint in the same direction you would normally. For instance, when painting cherries, follow the rounded horizontal contour of the fruit. On apples, the paint would be applied vertically, pulling from top to bottom. You may find it easier to undercoat only a few items at one time. Here's why. Fruit often overlaps each other. By undercoating the fruit that is underneath first and allowing it to dry, you may then use the wipe-out brush and turpentine when undercoating succeeding fruit without disturbing your other work.

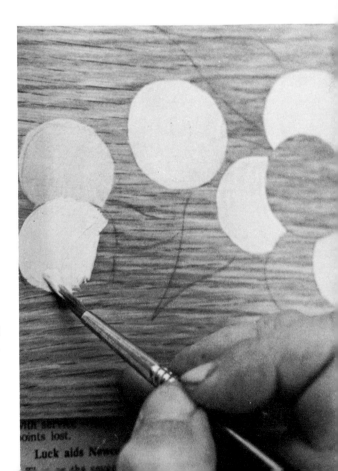

When fruit overlaps, undercoat bottom fruit first.

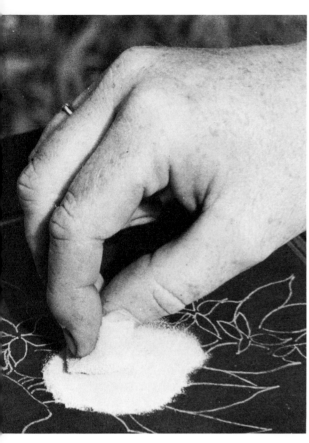

Pitty-pat with a sponge for realistic fruit texture.

Use the wipe-out brush to reshape sponged fruit.

Painting by Charlene Messerle.

An undercoat that is applied with a sponge is just as easy. Use one-inch cubes of synthetic sponge (cut from foam-rubber-pillow sponge, art foam, etc.). Dip the sponge in the undercoat, then pitty-pat onto the pattern. A sponged undercoat is desirable on fruits that are heavily textured, such as citrus fruits, peaches, and apricots.

Because a sponge is harder to control than a brush, you are sure to spread paint beyond the pattern line. Use the wipe-out brush to remove excess paint and reshape the fruit. If the wipe-out brush also removes part of the traced pattern, you may retrace the pattern or simpy refer to the pattern as a guide when you paint.

Sponging is fun! You may even decide to sponge some patterns that don't require an undercoat. Animal fur, human skin, fanciful designs, and clothing are all very effective when sponged instead of brushed. Using whipped-cream consistency paint, pat the sponge onto the pattern until the design is completely covered and remove excess paint with the wipe-out brush.

Whether you use a sponge or a brush should be determined by the texture you desire. For example, on the Raggedy Ann scarecrow shown, the artist sponged the face and cap. But the regular brush was used to create properly textured straw arms, raggedy dress, bow streamers, and pole. By giving a little thought to texture, you too can create beautiful tolework.

Chapter 4

Favorite Flower Patterns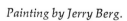

Just like yesteryear's painters, today's tole artists find flowers a favorite subject. Why? They're bright, cheerful, and—best yet—there's a flower to match every stage of painting skill. Daisies, for example, are preferred by beginners because each petal is created with a single basic stroke. With practice, you may wish to paint a flower with overlapping strokes, such as the chrysanthemum. And, when you're adept at color blending and shading, the poppy will be a must-try pattern.

However, even expert tole painters create the simple daisy again and again—for the daisy becomes more lovely with every try. See for yourself!

The Daisy

To paint a daisy, simply make a circle of basic strokes. That's really all there is to it—except that the circle shape will be more pleasing if you first paint the top strokes, then the bottom, then fill in the middle. Note that the top and bottom strokes are nearly straight, while middle strokes curve slightly in either direction. Naturally, you will need to turn and twist the object you are painting so that your hand will be in the best position to create each stroke.

White is the favorite daisy color. It may later be shaded with burnt umber antiquing. Or, you may shade by color-blending as you paint with yellow, green, or umber. If you prefer fanciful daisies, load the brush with white, dip the tip into red, and you'll have a "pinkish" daisy.

Painting by Jerry Berg.

26

Daisy pattern.

Paint top and bottom strokes, then fill in middle.

2 1
3
4
5
10
8 9
6 7

After all the daisy petals have been painted, make a yellow daisy center. Goop a small mound of paint into the center, then prick with the end of your brush to give it texture. Tiny strokes of burnt sienna may be placed in a half-circle around the center for additional dimension.

Leaves are next. Color-blend yellow green and permanent light green into your favorite leaf shape. Stems may be added with the liner using a thin mixture of burnt sienna.

Queen Anne's Lace

This delicate design is merely a combination of dots and the basic stroke that can be painted very quickly. But flowers arranged to complement the shape of the board and the well-formed strokes transform the simplicity into elegance.

When painting Queen Anne's lace, don't be satisfied with less than your best work. Remove poorly shaped strokes with the wipe-out brush dipped in turpentine and try again. To prevent smearing your work, paint from the top downward. When changing colors (like switching from leaves to dots), wipe the brush clean on tissue paper, dunk in turpentine, wipe dry, then load the brush with the new color.

Although the illustrated plaque is very impressive with white flowers, blue underpetals, and color-blended yellow green—permanent light green leaves, this is a good pattern for color experimentation. Flowers may be different shades of pastels, or they may be various hues of the same color. To create different hues, simply mix the chosen color with increasingly greater amounts of white.

Painting by Janet Lockhart.

Queen Anne's Lace pattern.

30

Allow balls to dry before adding basic stroke petals.

Painting by B. Kay Fraser.

Tole Flowers

Tole flowers, or folk-art flowers, are borrowed from early American painters. They rely on the basic stroke, of course, and are therefore easy to create.

Unlike the daisy and Queen Anne's lace, however, tole flowers are painted in two stages. First the "underneath" portion of the flower, such as the round ball, is painted and allowed to dry. Then, the basic stroke petals, crosshatching, and squiggles are added. Trying to paint the entire flower in one sitting can result in disaster, for the overlapping petals will smear the underneath portion.

The ball portion of the flower provides a good opportunity to try the sponging trick explained in Chapter 3. A tiny sponge will give the ball a nubbly texture. The remaining basic stroke petals are lovely when color-blended. For example, if you wish yellow flower petals, shade with yellow ochre and highlight with white. On the tole flowers shown, the artist chose red for the basic color—shading with alizarin crimson and adding highlight with white.

Tole flower pattern.

*Painting by
Janet Lockhart.*

Decorative Tole Flowers

Remember that in Chapter 1 it was pointed out that today's tole art is much more sophisticated than yesteryear's. As a good example, notice the excellent shading and beautifully arranged pattern of this plaque as compared to the preceding tole flowers.

This pattern should also be painted in two sessions, with the underneath portions of the flowers created first. Leaves and daisies may be painted during either session. Save the overlapping strokes, center stem, and bow until last.

Now, about that bow—a little bit of shading will make the bow appear real as life. On small bows, you may color-blend each stroke. On larger bows, it will be more effective to apply a dark shade of color on one side of the bow and a light shade on the other side. Then softly blend the two colors with your brush until color goes gradually from light to dark. Paint the bow turns first, then the streamers, and finally the knot.

If you know where this plaque will be hung, choose colors that will blend with the room's decor. If not, try painting it in autumn colors. On the plaque shown, the artist selected a mustard base color; orange, yellow, ochre, and sienna for main design colors; and burnt umber for antiquing.

*Decorative tole
flower pattern.*

Painting by B. Kay Fraser.

Chrysanthemums

"Mum" is really the word among tole painters because chrysanthemums are so impressive on door panels, trays, and plaques. Mums look a bit overpowering to paint because they are large, but take a closer look. Mums are actually basic stroke upon basic stroke!

To create chrysanthemums, first arrange the full mum, half mum, and bud in any way that pleases your eye, and trace onto the object. Your favorite leaves may then be traced. Next, select the basic color of the mum—perhaps white, yellow, even lavender. Shading and highlighting this basic color will give realism.

For example, if you choose white, you may shade with permanent light green, leaving some petals stark white for highlight. Yellow green makes a lovely ball center with white. Yellow mums may be shaded with ochre and highlighted with white; mix ochre and sienna for the ball center. A mixture of prussian blue and alizarin crimson may be used for ball centers with lavender mums. Keep part of this deep purple mixture for shading, and add white to the rest of the mixture to obtain lavender. Highlight with white.

When the colors have been chosen and mixed, first sponge in the ball center. Then paint the top petals, next front petals, and finally bottom petals. As you paint, use more shading on petals that are farther away, such as the top petals and petals that are underneath other petals. Petals that are closer to you, such as the very front petals, should be highlighted. Do not clean your brush as you change from dark to light colors. By leaving some of the old color on the brush, the change from dark to light will be gradual and very, very elegant.

By this time, you are probably a careful enough worker to paint the leaves without smearing the mums. However, it is always safer to let the mums dry before adding leaves than to risk smearing your still-wet work. Long green leaves are effective in permanent light green tipped with yellow green.

If you care to add more leaves, a darker color is suggested, such as viridian green highlighted with permanent light green and an occasional hint of yellow green. Or, if you are ready to experiment, try creating leaves in burnt umber color blended with yellow.

Chrysanthemum pattern.

Sunflowers

Sunflowers are easier to paint than chrysanthemums because the pattern is more exact. You can see which petals are underneath, and therefore know exactly which petals to shade. But sunflowers require far greater control of the brush. You must have the "feel" of when to press the brush firmly and when to release that pressure. This feel comes with experience, so do not attempt sunflowers until you have already completed at least two other patterns. You may try sunflowers with less experience, but you will probably spend more time wiping off mistakes than tole painting!

Sunflower colors are light yellow to medium yellow and a dab of burnt sienna. Paint the underneath petals first, using darker colors. Then gradually lighten the petals until the top petals are light yellow. As with chrysanthemums, there is no need to clean the brush between colors because the blending of dark and light is very effective.

You may let the sunflowers dry or continue to paint leaves and centers. Dark centers of sienna or burnt umber will match nature's own; gob the paint on and prick with the end of the brush for texture, as you did with daisy centers. Dark leaves, such as viridian green tipped with yellow green or burnt umber blended with yellow, are recommended.

Painting by Sylvia Sauter.

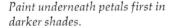

Paint underneath petals first in darker shades.

Sunflower pattern.

Painting by Sylvia Sauter.

Dogwood Flowers

Dogwood flowers appear simple to paint, and they are. But you will use two new techniques. For example, dogwood leaves are underneath the flower and therefore should be painted first. Because the flowers are so light, it makes a nice contrast to paint leaves in flat, "blah" colors. Try muddying permanent light green and yellow green with a dab of burnt umber, then color-blend. Add a vein to the leaf in burnt umber.

When the leaves have dried, you may try the second new technique—using the wipe-out brush to paint with rather than your regular brush. The flat edge of the wipe-out brush gives a realistic edge to dogwood flower petals. Using white, paint from the outside of the petal toward the center. As with daisies, you may later antique to get the proper shading; or you may shade as you paint with a hint of raw umber. Petal edges and centers should be more deeply shaded. The flower center itself is made entirely of little dots. Dots may be yellow green or yellow or a combination of the two, and are easy to create with the tip of the liner brush.

If you are a tole painter who likes to combine patterns, keep this flower in mind when painting fruit. Dogwood flowers complement cherries, apples, strawberries—any bright-colored fruit.

Dogwood flower pattern.

Painting by Sylvia Sauter.

Roses

At some time in your tole painting life, you will probably want to try everybody's favorite—the rose. But the rose is no snap. Unless rose petals are carefully shaded and highlighted, this flower can easily turn into a formless blob.

The secret of a nice rose is to mix a variety of hues in your chosen color. For example, if you want a pink rose, you should have alizarin crimson, red, white, and at least two shades in between on your palette. As you paint the rose—beginning at the base, of course—keep more of the darker color in your brush. As you swirl your way from bottom to top, pick up increasingly more lighter color in the brush until the tip is nearly pure white. And you'll have a pink rose!

Another way to create a rose is to think of it as a cup and saucer. The base is the saucer, and each petal here is shaded from light to dark. The light part is the edge, and the darkest part adjoins the cup. The inside of the cup is painted next—very light on top and increasingly darker as it goes into the

Painting by Janet Lockhart.

Rose pattern.

flower center. Finally, paint the outside cup. The bottom of the cup will be darkest where it touches the saucer and becomes lighter as you paint your way up to the flower center.

Rosebuds are made with several strokes of the full rose color and surrounding strokes in the leaf color.

Most tole painters find that roses combine beautifully with white flowers, such as dogwood and daisies. If you want to combine your roses into a more elaborate arrangement than the pattern shown, simply trace flowers from the daisy and dogwood patterns and arrange to your satisfaction. With more elaborate arrangements, you must plan ahead, for underneath flowers and leaves should always be painted first and allowed to dry before adding flowers that go "on top."

The Poppy

The beautiful poppy is a "no-no" unless you have already successfully completed three or four other flowers. Granted, no one is there to slap your hands. But unless you are familiar with shading, pattern arrangement, and have good control of the brush, poppies will be a frustrating experience, and the purpose of tole painting is to have fun.

If, however, you now have tole-painted daisies, chrysanthemums, and roses cheering your home, then you're ready to try the most challenging, lushest flower of all—the poppy. As with mums, the poppies must first be arranged to complement the object you are painting. As with dogwood, the

Painting by Sylvia Sauter.

Poppy pattern.

leaves and buds should be painted first in rich, dark greens or umber and yellow. And, as with roses, a variety of hues should be premixed on the palette, then color-blended as you paint.

The suggested basic color is orange, highlighted in yellow and shaded with sienna. Or, instead of using orange, you may stroke first in red then in cadmium yellow to get an orange effect. When painting poppies, let the photograph be your guide. Note how the outside edges are very light, the inside very dark. The artist created this contrast by shading as she painted—the poppies were not antiqued!

When the poppies have dried, the edges may be tipped in pure yellow; this makes the petal appear to be "turning." Now you may also add the daisies and poppy centers. Centers are made with the liner—first make dots of yellow and yellow green, then add burnt umber fibers.

The final step is to place your tole-painted poppies in a very conspicuous place. You'll deserve all the compliments they will bring!

Chapter 5

Fruit and
Vegetable Designs

Tole-painted fruit and vegetables look yummy enough to eat! But during the painting process, the only thing you'll want to chew are your fingernails. For painting fruit and vegetables requires time, patience, and great care. In fact, it may take up to six different painting sessions to complete a mixed-fruit pattern. But it will be worth the effort. Tole-painted fruit is so realistic, so lovely to look at, that many tole artists will paint nothing else.

Although fruit and vegetables do take more time than other designs, they are really just as simple. You still have patterns to depend upon, and you still use the basic stroke for leaves and flowers. The main difference between painting fruit and painting other designs is that fruit should be undercoated, as explained in Chapter 3. This undercoat gives fruit and vegetables extra depth and texture.

Another difference is that you will often paint with a sponge instead of a brush, a procedure also explained in Chapter 3. A sponge is used for fruits of rough texture, such as lemons and peaches. The regular brush will be used for strawberries and cherries, although many artists prefer to use the wipe-out brush on apples.

Thus, the difference between painting fruit and painting flowers is actually very little. Let's try it!

Apples

Apples are an excellent fruit to start with because by painting them, you will learn the basics of all painted fruit. First, undercoat the apple that is

Apply suggested colors, then blend with a brush.

Painting by Charlene Messerle.

underneath. Using the wipe-out brush, pull the paint from top to bottom, following the contours of the apple. Wipe off any paint that goes outside the pattern line, including paint that overlaps the top apple. After the bottom apple dries, undercoat the top apple. By first allowing the bottom apple to dry, you may again remove paint that goes outside the line without smearing the bottom apple. Let the top apple dry.

Now you can apply those yummy apple colors, again beginning with the bottom apple. When making green apples, outline the apple with burnt umber. Make another ring inside it of umber mixed with yellow ochre. Fill in the center with yellow green. Next, make three V's in the upper center with yellow, yellow green, and umber. Blend these colors, pulling from top to bottom with the wipe-out brush. If desired, you may add additional highlight by blending a dab of yellow or white in the center of the apple. This blending of color will result in an apple ready to bite. When dry, paint the top apple.

If you prefer red apples, follow the same procedure, using alizarin crimson mixed with a small amount of burnt umber for the outline. The inside ring is crimson mixed with red. Fill the center with red, and make V's with these three color mixtures. Yellow or white may be blended in the center for extra highlight.

After the apples have dried, add leaves and branches. Squiggly branches are painted with the regular brush. Use yellow ochre for the basic color; shade with burnt umber; and highlight with white.

Apple pattern.

48

*Painting by
B. Kay Fraser.*

Lemons

Citrus fruits are a wise choice for your second fruit pattern. You undercoat, blend colors for realism, and finally add branches and leaves the same way you did on apples. But with lemons, you will use a sponge to blend colors instead of a brush.

First, undercoat each lemon with a sponge, allowing it to dry before adding the next lemon. When painting the lemon, apply yellow ochre to edges that go beneath other lemons (for shading); fill in with lemon yellow; add white to the center (for highlight); and place a spot of yellow green on the tip. Now blend by pitty-patting the sponge from the outside into the center. When dry, the lemon will not only look like a real lemon, but it will feel like a lemon too!

To give this lemon pattern added dimension, keep the bottom lemon darker by using more ochre and the top lemon lighter by using more white. You'll see why—darker fruit appears farther away, while light fruit seems closest to you.

The branch is painted with the same colors used for the apple branch. Lemon leaves are lovely when yellow green and permanent light green are blended.

If you prefer limes to lemons, use yellow green for the basic color. Shade with permanent light green and highlight with white or lemon yellow.

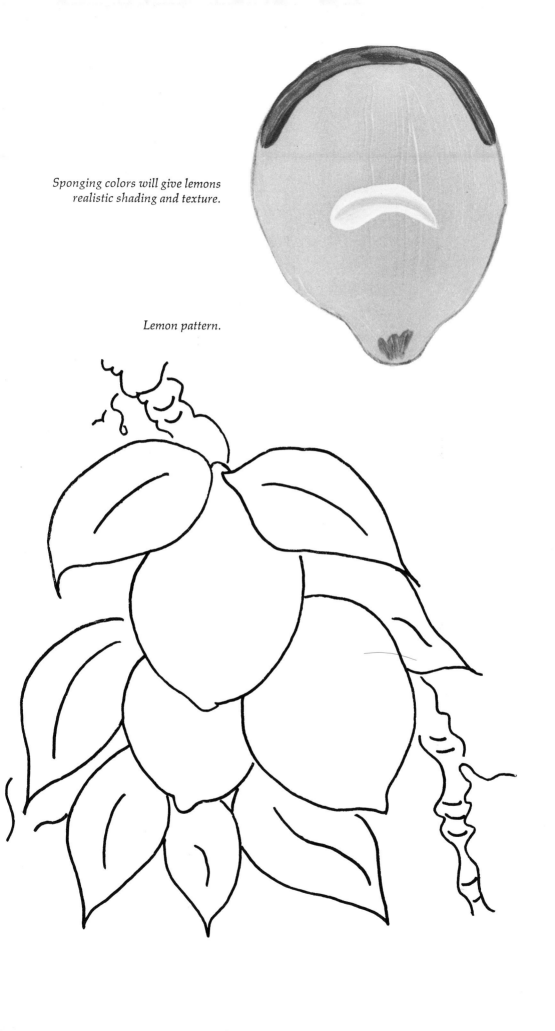

Sponging colors will give lemons realistic shading and texture.

Lemon pattern.

Painting by Janet Lockhart.

Carefully blend colors, sponging one half at a time.

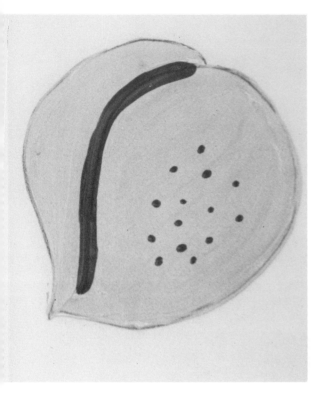

Peaches

Sponging also creates lovely peaches and apricots—but do pitty-pat more gently on these fruits because you're aiming for a fuzz texture rather than a coarse lemon rind.

Again, undercoating is recommended, although with this pattern you may undercoat two peaches at a time (two underneath ones first). To give your peach true-as-nature color, fill in the peach in cadmium yellow. Make a long red stroke that follows the center line. Add red dots for shading. Now, carefully, carefully (yes, doubly carefully!) sponge the left-hand side of the peach first, blending the red line into the yellow. The line itself should be practically pure red, while the outside edge is nearly solid yellow. Next, blend the left half of the peach with a clean sponge moving from the center toward the outside edge. Do not touch the red line with the sponge.

Granted, sponging a peach is more tedious than sponging a lemon, but your efforts will be rewarded with a really luscious-looking peach. Use the same technique for apricots, only substitute orange for red (or, substitute white for yellow).

Peach pattern.

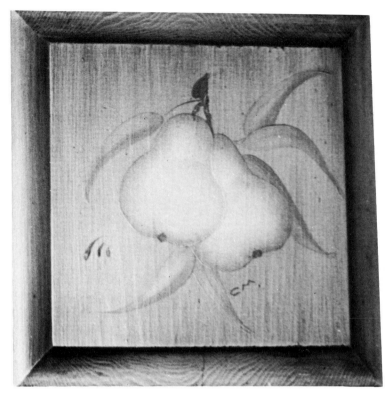

Painting by Charlene Messerle.

Pears

One more fruit relies upon sponging for its natural look—the pear. But it will only look natural if you sponge lightly, for the pear has a nearly smooth skin.

After the undercoat has dried, outline the pear and curve in burnt sienna. Make a second line of yellow ochre. Fill the inside of the pear with lemon yellow. Add a few red dots to the pear's center. Blend colors by sponging from the outside line toward the center. Begin with the top half of the pear, then follow the line all the way around into the inside curve. Use a clean sponge whenever you find you are blending too much dark color into the light. If the color becomes too light or too dark, that problem is easily remedied by adding either more yellow (light) or more ochre (dark) to the sponge and blending in.

When the pear has dried, add burnt sienna stem and blossom fibers. Leaves are impressive in viridian green tipped with yellow green.

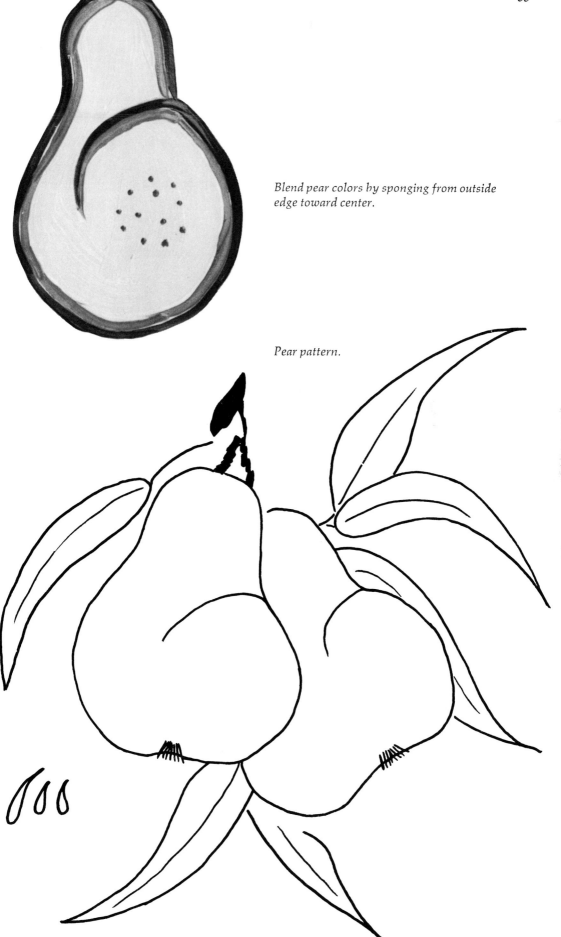

Blend pear colors by sponging from outside edge toward center.

Pear pattern.

*Cherries are created with red,
alizarin crimson, and white.*

Painting by B. Kay Fraser.

Cherries

Meanwhile, back to the brush! Cherries are more satiny smooth and delicate when painted with a brush because you can pull the paint into the same rounded contour as Mother Nature creates.

After undercoating, paint the underneath cherries first. Make a ball of red, adding a touch of white to the center for highlight and dab of alizarin crimson on top for shading. Underneath cherries should have more shading, while top cherries should have more highlight. The colors may be blended, pulling from one side to the other, with the regular brush. However, you will have a smoother cherry if you gently sweep the wipe-out brush across the fruit in several half-moon motions. The bristles should barely touch the paint—just enough to blend the colors. This flat-edged brush will leave barely perceptible lines, whereas the regular brush often leaves definite ridges.

When all the cherries are painted and dry, add the leaves, keeping underneath leaves darker than those on top. Stems are made with the liner brush dipped in both yellow green and burnt umber. An additional swirl of alizarin crimson may be added at the stem base for extra depth.

Cherry pattern.

Strawberry colors are blended by brushing from bottom to top, left to right.

Strawberries

You're going to love strawberries—they're fun to paint, fun to look at, and fun to hang on kitchen walls. One tole painter even painted huge strawberries on her daughter's bedstead. So, learn the basics and apply your berries where you will.

Because bright red berries are so lovely with white flowers and dark green leaves, let's try a more elaborate arrangement of fruit. First, paint the leaves, highlighting the left side of the leaf. Pretend that the sun is shining in such a way that the left side is in the sun, the right side in the shade. And don't forget which way the sun is shining when you highlight your berries!

When the leaves have dried, undercoat the berries. The regular brush should be pulled vertically from bottom to top, swinging the brush left or right to fill in the top of the berry. Use the same motions when applying the final berry colors—red, shaded with alizarin crimson, highlighted with a stroke of white, and tipped with yellow green. Start on the left side so that the brush will first pick up the dark color, blending it into the red, then the red will gradually merge with the white, etc.

When the berries are dry, cap with five basic strokes in permanent green and yellow green. Berry seeds are color-blended yellow and burnt sienna. Now you may also add the white flowers, which you learned how to paint in Chapter 4. The squiggles are created with a thin mixture of burnt sienna using the liner brush.

On the strawberry pattern illustrated, the artist skillfully used antiquing glaze to give her strawberries additional depth. Using a cotton swab, she removed glaze from the highlighted side of berries and leaves, leaving more glaze on the shaded side.

Painting by Carolyn Nordahl.

Strawberry pattern.

*A little paint and a little finger
create realistic grapes.*

*Painting by
B. Kay Fraser.*

Grapes

Pity the poor grape! It is rarely painted by itself, but always must share the limelight with other fruit. To make matters worse, the grape is often discussed in tole-painting circles with such words as "ugh" and "ick." The reason is that grapes are not painted with a few choice strokes, such as the apple or cherry. Rather, grapes are composed of seemingly endless circle upon circle.

But grapes are truly beautiful and an enhancement to any fruit design, so let's begin the dirty work. (Yes, dirty—you use your little finger!) On the pattern shown, begin by undercoating the apricots; add leaves; then paint apricots as explained under "Peaches."

Now, we're ready for grapes. Outline in prussian blue mixed lightly with payne's grey. Fill in the center with prussian blue and dot with white. Rub the mixture into a well-shaped circle with your little finger. Wipe off paint that goes outside the pattern line. Grapes that are underneath should be darker, so use more prussian blue. Top grapes are lighter, requiring more white. Start with grapes that are underneath and work your way to the grapes on top.

This is the easiest method of painting grapes. But there is another way. You may first undercoat each grape. Then, using the same colors, gently swirl the wipe-out brush in a circle to give the grape shape rather than using your finger. Or, if you prefer more "purply" grapes, substitute magenta for prussian blue.

Perhaps you want green grapes. Using the same technique, apply yellow green for the base color, permanent green mixed with burnt umber for shading and white for highlight.

Grape and apricot pattern.

Mixed fruit is delightful on unusual objects. Painting by Carolyn Nordahl.

Painting by B. Kay Fraser.

Mixed Fruit

Although the grapes mixed with apricots gave you an inkling of the time-taking task of creating mixed fruit, it was just the beginning! Patterns that boast an assortment of fruit require a great deal of patience, but these patterns are absolutely breathtaking.

Mixed fruit is so lovely that it is painted on prized antiques, expensive cabinets, favorite picnic baskets—just about anything you can think of. Play it safe on your first mixed-fruit design, however, by using a cutting board (only a dollar or two at the variety store). Suggested base colors are olive green, muted gold, or natural wood.

The first step in creating mixed fruit is to decide what must be under-coated first. For example, on the pattern shown, the peach, apple, underneath cherry, and underneath apricot could all be undercoated in the first painting session. When dry, undercoat the pear, strawberry, top cherry, and top apricot. In addition, if you plan to undercoat the grapes, they must be painted accordingly—underneath grapes first.

After all undercoating is completed, paint the leaves. Dark, thin paint is recommended because you want the fruit to catch the eye, not the leaves. Remember where the sun is "shining" when highlighting your leaves.

Mixed fruit pattern.

At last you may paint the fruit colors, using the same plan of attack that you used when undercoating. When all fruit has dried, add stems, flowers, squiggle, berry cap and seeds, pear and apple blossom fibers.

You're through! It was a long process—but wasn't it worth the effort? Now, keep this cutting board for your guide when you paint more treasured objects. It will not only cheer your kitchen wall but the backside may still be used as a cutting board if you leave it natural. Some tole artists claim that three coats of plastic varnish in addition to the usual two coats of regular varnish will protect the design from cutting blades. (Personally, I've never had the nerve to risk it!)

Mushrooms

Mushrooms are perhaps the funnest pattern of all—and certainly one of the easiest. Mushrooms require no undercoating, they can be painted in one session, and are impressive on ornate plaques or driftwood.

When painting mushrooms, the first step is to paint the cap. Use a bright-colored paint and gob it onto the cap. Spread the paint to fill the pattern with a brush, following the contour of the cap. This leaves nice bumpy ridges. Next, paint the underside of the mushroom and the stem, again pulling the brush in the direction of the mushroom's natural shape. Stem colors may be in contrast to the cap, or you may mix white with the cap color to get a lighter shade. Finally, add flowers, grass, butterflies, ladybugs, or frogs.

You will notice that the mushrooms shown have been outlined for emphasis. If you have a steady, sure hand, the outline may be added during the same painting session. If not, wait until the paint has dried to add outlines of burnt sienna or payne's gray.

Because mushrooms are usually painted in gay fanciful colors—such as lemon yellow, orange, red, yellow green—antiquing is needed to subdue the bright tones. Burnt umber is the most commonly used oil in the antiquing glaze.

Painting by B. Kay Fraser.

Painting by Jerry Berg.

Mushroom patterns.

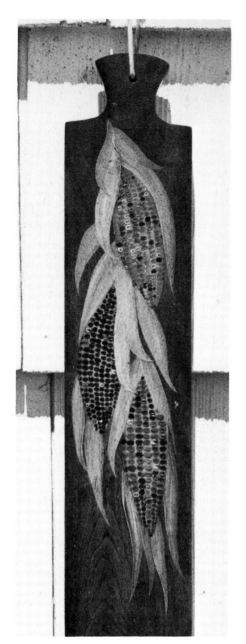

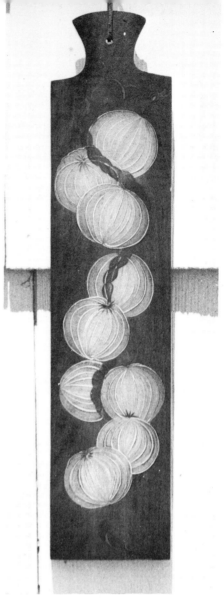

Paintings by Charlene Messerle.

Corn and Onions

Because corn and onions can be so cleverly arranged on long paddles and French-bread cutting boards, they make a practical as well as beautiful addition to kitchen walls.

After arranging corn to please your eye, paint the kernels, using the flat-edged wipe-out brush. You may use corn fresh from the field as your guide, alternating cadmium yellow, lemon yellow, and white to achieve nature's colors. The leaves would then be a yellow green color blended with white. However, the artist whose work is illustrated selected the autumn colors of Indian corn to make her eye-catching arrangement. Kernels are burnt sienna, cadmium yellow, and an occasional white and orange kernel. Leaves were created (after the kernels had dried) with burnt umber plentifully highlighted with white.

Corn and onion patterns.

Onions are much less tedious to create than corn, but you will notice that careful control of the brush is a "must" to create the lovely ridges. Using white shaded with raw umber, paint underneath onions first. By now you are probably adept enough with your brush that you do not need to wait for the underneath onions to dry. So continue painting until all the onions are completed.

When dry, add blossom fibers in burnt sienna and perhaps add a twisting stem in burnt sienna highlighted with yellow ochre. Careful shading as you paint will eliminate the need for antiquing.

Corn and onion paddles look dandy hung from a leather thong. A pair of leather shoelaces for boots will provide enough thongs for at least half a dozen paddles.

Painting by Francie Richardson.

Mixed Vegetables

Although vegetables are never sponged, they are created the same as fruit in many ways. For example, undercoating is recommended; basic colors are highlighted and shaded; and antiquing is certain to enhance the design.

Start with carrots. This vegetable is most natural in orange highlighted with yellow and shaded with the antiquing glaze. Fill in the carrot with orange, placing tiny strokes of lemon yellow where the "sun shines." Then gently swipe the wipe-out brush in half-moons across the carrot to blend the colors and pull the paint in the natural direction. (You used the same technique on cherries.) Clean the wipe-out brush in turpentine, then use it to remove paint that went outside the pattern line. Leaves may be sponged in green and yellow green, or use the liner to make short, choppy strokes that will resemble carrot leaves.

Radishes will look yummy enough to bite if you first paint the whole radish with white. Fill the wipe-out brush with red and pull from top to middle. This flat edge brush will give a streaked effect where red blends with white. Leaves are permanent green shaded with viridian green and highlighted with white.

Now, about those peas. Whole pods are painted from stem end to tip in yellow green that has been toned down with white and a dab of burnt umber. Highlight one side of the pod with more white and shade the other with more umber. The same colors are used on open pods except that the background for the round peas is very dark—almost pure burnt umber. When dry, add round peas in the basic color of the pod. Highlight with white. Pea leaves can be made with permanent green highlighted with yellow green.

Any vegetable can be created by simply using it as your model. Try to duplicate its natural colors and shading. On a pepper, for example, the front portion would naturally be a lighter green, and each receding portion a bit darker. The brush would be pulled from top to bottom, swinging slightly to follow the vegetable's contour. Pluck other vegetables from your garden or grocery counter and see for yourself how much fun it is to duplicate Nature.

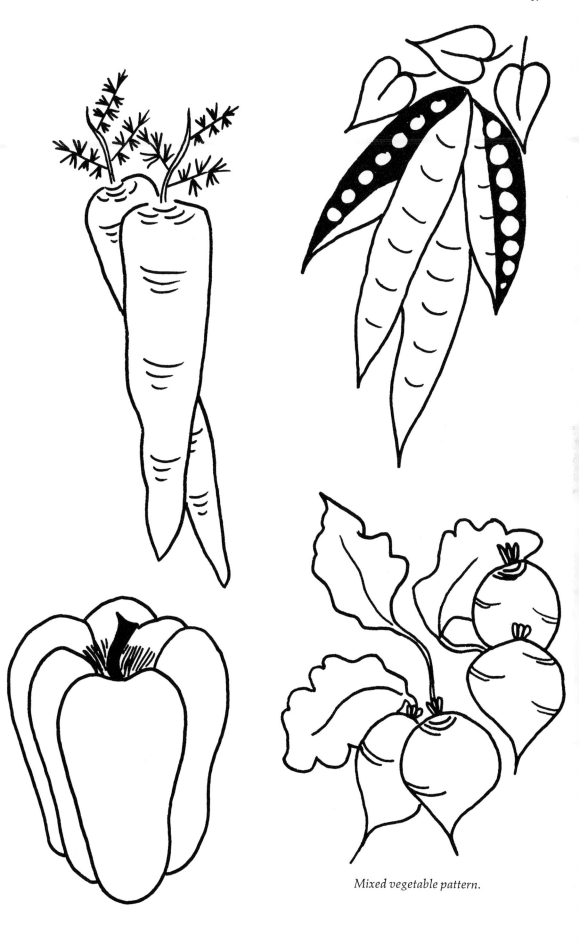

Mixed vegetable pattern.

Chapter 6

Fun with Birds, Animals, Children

The patterns presented in this chapter offer the opportunity to let your imagination soar. Birds, animals, and children should be painted in favorite, fun colors. Use the pattern as a guide only, for you're free to add flowers, decorative accents—any personal touch that will make the painting individually yours!

The Federal Eagle

The federal eagle, first painted by early American artists to symbolize their love of freedom, remains the most popular of all tole designs. There are variations of the eagle, of course. Some artists show the eagle with outspread

Painting by Jerry Berg.

Federal eagle pattern.

wings; some have the eagle perched on a flag; others place an olive branch in the eagle's beak. The splendid eagle shown was adapted from an eagle first used as an oval inlay by an eighteenth-century cabinetmaker.

The principles of tole painting an eagle remain the same, whatever design is chosen. For example, the wings must first be painted beginning at the wing bottom. Use white shaded with either raw umber or burnt sienna. As you can see, the wing is created of basic stroke upon basic stroke. Use the same method to create the neck, leg, and tail feathers. Add a gray beak and talons (mix payne's gray with white for a nice gray color).

When dry, add a shield of prussian blue, red, and white; an eye of white and payne's gray; arrows of ochre and payne's gray; olive branch of yellow green and permanent light green; and red stars.

Painting by Jerry Berg.

Little Lovebirds

More fanciful than the eagle, but still a remnant of early American folk art, are the precious little lovebirds.

Here are a few tips on painting the birds . . . but your imagination must supply the tole flowers and decorative accents! Birds may be either sponged or brushed, then basic stroke feathers added. The bird in back should be painted first in a darker color. For example, on the plaque shown, the artist chose yellow green for the behind bird and lemon yellow for the bird in front. Add the birds' legs; if desired, outline the birds for emphasis; then try your creative hand at added decoration.

Little lovebirds pattern.

Painting by Charlene Messerle.

A Laying Hen

Naturally, hens were a favorite design of early settlers for they represented fertility as well as abundant food. It may be difficult to appreciate this symbolism if you buy eggs in a carton at the store! But it won't be difficult to appreciate the beauty of a laying hen when created with careful brush strokes.

The design shown may be painted in an evening—if you're careful not to smear. First sponge in the egg, using white shaded with raw umber. Next, fill in the hen's shape and tail feathers, using burnt sienna. Then add basic stroke feathers of red, payne's gray, and cadmium yellow. The comb is red, the beak yellow, and the eye white and payne's gray. Hay is created with short, choppy strokes of the liner brush in yellow, sienna, and payne's gray.

Remember, color suggestions are only *suggestions*. Don't overlook the fun of experimenting with your own color ideas.

Laying hen design.

Paintings by Sylvia Sauter.

Contemporary Owls

Now, switching from yesteryear's favorite birds to today's we find owls extremely popular—and easy!

First, paint in branches with sienna highlighted in ochre and perhaps a touch of white. Then paint the owl's tummy, using basic stroke upon basic stroke in white shaded with raw umber. Next, paint wings and head in sienna highlighted with yellow. Use more sienna around the ears and eyes for extra shading. The face is again white shaded with raw umber. Finally, paint eyes and beak—and by now, you should know which colors to use!

Leaves may be added in yellow green and permanent light green.

Because contemporary owls are so lovable and fun, they are often painted on unusual objects, such as driftwood and rocks (which are used as paperweights). The surface of such items will not be smooth and therefore your brush strokes will be more difficult to create. However, this is one of the rare times when you may use a spray varnish to help seal the surface before tole painting.

Contemporary owl designs.

Paintings by Chris Messerle.

Fanciful Animals

Children's rooms can be cheered with fanciful animals. Select animals they know and like, such as a tiger from a cereal box, a crocodile from a favorite storybook, or a bear from a popular children's television program. As explained in Chapter 3, you can make any pattern with pencil and tracing paper.

Children adore bright colors. Therefore, you'll delight them more with animals shaded as you paint rather than dulled by antiquing glaze. Thus you must carefully select a base coat that complements the design. Base-coat colors often used for children's plaques are white, natural light yellow, baby blue, soft green, and powder pink.

Animals may be sponged rather than painted. Sponging gives a more furry texture. Because children will love to touch your animals, be sure to protect the painting with ample coats of varnish.

Animal patterns.

A Young Lad

Little boys are precious when tole painted with characteristic mannerisms, such as an unhappy expression when practicing the violin, or shoelaces that never stay tied. An excellent source of little boy patterns is greeting cards. As you learned in Chapter 3, patterns taken from cards may be enlarged or reduced to fit the object you are painting by squaring off the design.

When painting young lads, use appropriate bright, contrasting colors. For example, the artist whose work is shown selected red for the shirt, green pants, blue cap, yellow hair, and outlined for emphasis in payne's gray. If you do select a pattern from a greeting card, you will find excellent color suggestions on the card itself.

Spread the word among your friends that you use cards for patterns, and you'll soon have more greeting cards than you could ever use in one tole-painting lifetime!

Little boy design.

Painting by Jerry Berg.

Painting by B. Kay Fraser.

*Painting by
Charlene Messerle.*

A Little Girl

Although contemporary greeting cards may be used for patterns, tole painting is still a folk art. Each artist creates the pattern a bit differently.

As a good example, the pattern shown originally had a big bug on the hat and no daisies. One artist added the daisies, the other added a bee. One artist painted a brunette white girl, using shading for contrast, while the other artist decided upon a black girl and outlined for contrast. And each painter chose completely different color combinations.

Even the size of the pattern in relation to the board differs. One artist preferred a large plaque carefully antiqued to enhance the design, while the other artist selected a smaller plaque and didn't antique at all.

Try painting this darling little girl yourself and prove how your individual ideas keep this a folk art even though we're all using the same basic pattern.

A little girl pattern.

Chapter 7

Patterns for
Special Occasions

A decorative tole plaque is the perfect gift. So why not go one step farther by painting a gift for that special occasion!

Marriage

The lucky couple who receives a tole-painted wedding invitation will be grateful throughout their wedded years. But you must start the plaque the minute the invitation arrives in the mail, or you won't complete it by the wedding date. Wedding-invitation plaques do take time!

The first step is to seal and base-coat the plaque as usual. Suggested colors are natural, olive green, or harvest gold. Next, cut the invitation to fit and glue it onto the plaque with a good paper glue or ready-made decoupage medium. Protect the invitation with at least two coats of satin-finish varnish.

Now you may either antique the plaque or tole paint before antiquing. Either way, antiquing is a *must*. The glaze will shade the invitation, making it look a natural part of the board rather than a piece of paper you just glued on.

Painting by Jerry Berg.

Wedding invitation pattern.

When the tole work and antiquing steps are finished, the plaque should be given at least three coats of varnish for extra protection from handling. Remember, the plaque must last a lifetime!

Anniversary

Whether young or young-at-heart, most couples will truly appreciate a contemporary lovebird on their anniversary. When painted in cheerful colors, this plaque is a gay reminder of that little four-letter word that keeps a marriage happy.

Bold, bright colors are recommended. For example, the artist first sponged in the background, using lavender. Then the letters were filled in with shock-

*Painting by
B. Kay Fraser.*

Contemporary lovebird design.

ing pink, light pink, red, and orange. Note how the paint was poked with the edge of the wipe-out brush to give the letters texture. Next, the border, legs, and hearts were painted in medium pink. The eye and branch were added in payne's gray. Finally, the tiny hearts were applied with two basic strokes of light pink. (Mix white with red to get various shades of pink.)

If you work carefully, you can complete the tolework within an hour. But it will bring many years of pleasure to the lucky recipients.

Painting by Charlene Messerle.

Christmas

If your holiday decorations are crumbling with age or if you want to delight friends with a special gift, then use your new hobby to paint Christmas plaques.

Simply use the patterns here or copy your own from favorite Christmas cards. When finished, staple plaques to a red velvet ribbon and hang from a golden curtain ring.

On the plaques illustrated, the artist chose a red base coat. The stocking, pears, angel's face, and gown were sponged. The ribbon, tree, bird, leaves, and angel's wings were applied with the regular brush. And the liner brush was needed to create the angel's hair and tiny decorative accents.

When finished, your Christmas plaque will enhance your holiday decor as well as give you a well-earned sense of accomplishment.

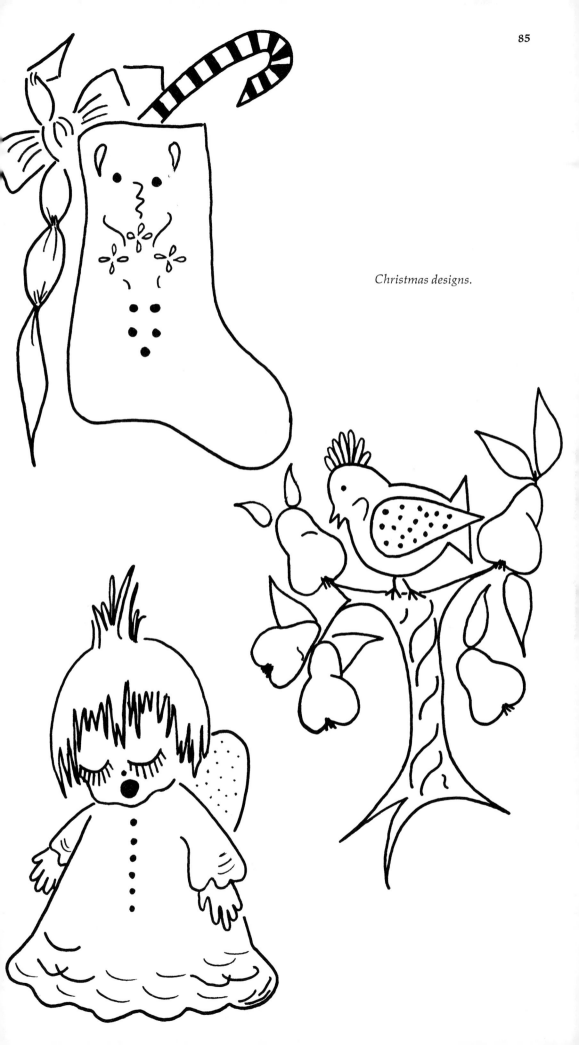

Christmas designs.

Painting by Julie Bower.

Valentine's Day

Valentine's Day is a good occasion to thrill a friend with a tole painted heart, a favorite design of early French settlers. Add tole flowers, birds, and carefully placed basic stroke accents. Presto—you'll have a pattern from yesteryear that still means love and friendship today!

Inspiration

Is a friend sick, a relative having a tough time on a diet, husband under strain on the job? No matter what the reason, folks will forget their troubles when they see your humorous message of inspiration. Or paint one for yourself (we all need a mental boost occasionally!).

Easily painted in an hour, the hippopotamus should first be sponged. Use a bright, cheery color. Add daisies with the regular brush. The liner will be needed to outline, letter, and to create stems and grass. If you have any leftover paint, use it to paint the edges of the plaque.

Painting by B. Kay Fraser.

French heart design.

Keep Your Chins Up!

Happy hippo pattern.

Friendship

A pleasant reminder that "somebody loves me" is this little berry plaque. It makes an especially nice gift for folks who live far away—nice thoughts can carry for miles!

Painting by B. Kay Fraser.

I love you pattern.

A two-session project, the basket and berries should be painted first. On the basket, use yellow shaded with red and sienna. Basket bands should be solid sienna. Berries may all be painted red, or alternate red and orange. When dry, add berry faces and leaves, ladybugs, basket trim, and lettering. When painting cheerful plaques, antiquing is not necessary.

New Home

A decorative plaque that wishes a family well makes an ideal house-warming gift. If you know the colors used in the new home's decor, use an accent color for the base coat. Antique before applying the design.

Paint the scroll in white, shading the scroll turns with raw umber. Add leaves of viridian green highlighted with yellow green. Follow the instructions in Chapter 4 to paint dogwood flowers or you can substitute daisies. When dry, add the lettering. For a truly personalized touch, you may substitute the family's name—such as "God Bless the Smiths."

Painting by Sylvia Sauter.

Scroll and dogwood design.

Chapter 8

On Your Own

If you've perfected the brush stroke and sampled many of the patterns, then already you're creating professional-looking tole art. So—where do you go from here? That's the joy of tole painting: there are always different techniques, various paints and brushes, and new patterns to present a challenge.

For example, you have seen in this book the work of tole painters on the central Oregon coast. But as tole painters of yesteryear varied techniques and patterns from colony to colony, so do today's painters. In the Midwest, tole painters often mix their artist's oils with turpentine and linseed oil instead of varnish. On the Eastern seaboard, tole painters tend to favor original folk art patterns rather than today's more sophisticated designs.

You see, there is no right or wrong to tole painting. It is still a folk art—and different folks discover different techniques that please them. Thus, you too are free to experiment. It's all part of the fun; but do keep a notebook, jotting down which techniques and experiments worked (and which didn't)!

And do keep an open mind to benefit from the experience of other tole painters. Tole-painting courses are available from individual artists, community colleges, and the Young Women's Christian Association. If, however, you have successfully completed most of the patterns shown, then you are capable of teaching a class yourself. So, before enrolling in a course, examine the instructor's work to make sure that you will actually be learning something new.

Or, if you know another tole painter, set up an afternoon session to swap techniques. Chances are you have learned some things other tole painters will want to try, and they know things you might want to try. Individual tole painters often group together, also, in pattern-exchanging parties. By learning to tole paint, you've not only become an artist, but you've opened the door to new friendships!

Developing a Style

When you first begin tole painting, you will probably adhere rigidly to directions and follow the pattern exactly. After your confidence has been boosted by a few successful tole paintings, however, you might begin to waver from the suggested colors and patterns. That's great! It's your special ideas that keep tole painting a folk art.

Actually, your tole painting tells a lot about your personality. For instance, persons who paint with gay colors and casually placed strokes are themselves often cheerful, happy-go-lucky people. Other artists, whose work is very, very careful and exact, are usually those marvelous people who remember birthdays and have impeccably clean homes. The point is that you, too, will develop a style that is uniquely YOU!

Developing a style is not a conscious process, though. Your style will come with practice and experimentation. You'll develop a preference for certain colors, special designs, particular objects—like decorative plaques or more practical items. In time, other tole painters will recognize your work for its special style, just as you will recognize theirs. As a test, thumb through the pattern chapters one year from today and see if you can tell who painted what without looking at the names.

Always Be Professional

The first time a friend offered to part with that lovely folding stuff if she could only have a tole painting she particularly admired, I was so flattered that I naturally gave it to her (free!) on the spot. Although I have sold numerous paintings since that time, I confess that a word of admiration means more to me than a greenback.

But the opportunity is there to sell your work—if you are less vulnerable to flattery than I am! Gift shops, restaurants, department stores, art centers, local fairs, and antique shops will often sell your work for a commission. Even if you don't sell your work, you'll find that friends and relatives appreciate your thoughtful tole-painted work as gifts much more than they would appreciate any store-bought item *if* . . .

Well, the *if* is so important that let's divide it into three parts. First *if* you always do your best work. If a basic stroke goes awry, if the antiquing glaze becomes smudged, if the color you chose doesn't contrast well—by all means wipe it off and start over. Never kid yourself that no one will be able to tell. Friends who don't tole paint can still recognize slipshod work.

Professional tole painters always finish the back of their work.

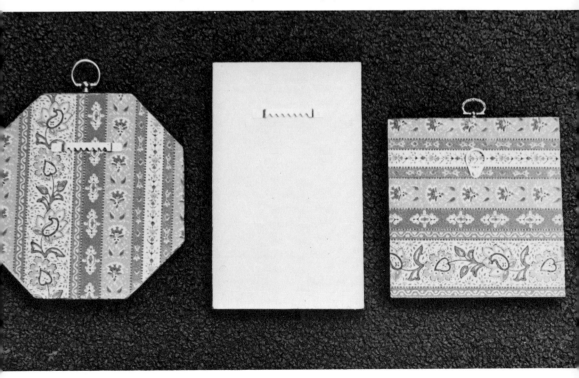

The second if is *if you sign your name*. After all, tole painting is an art, and you should sign your name or initials on every piece you paint. Who knows? Years from today, your work might be a collector's item! Some tole artists even sign the date under their initials. This is particularly thoughtful if the painting will be passed from generation to generation.

The final if is *if you create a work that is professional from start to finish*. This means, of course, that you must not become lazy about applying those endless coats of varnish. It means that you must guard your work from glunt (dust and lint) while drying. Even the most beautifully color-blended tole painting will look tacky if you allow glunt to settle on wet paint. In fact, the real pros dry their work on a card table that has been turned upside down and covered with a plastic sheet. Glunt can't reach it there.

Being professional from start to finish also means that you do *finish*. Paint and antique the underside and inside of buckets and milk cans. Paint the backside of decorative plaques or glue on wallpaper, then add decorative hooks from the hardware store. The actual hook should also be added for wall hanging, or tack on the pull-tops from beverage cans for hanging!

Even if you don't choose to go professional, you will still profit from decorative tole painting. Those tiny brush strokes that took hours to perfect will now bring hours of entertainment and relaxation. And just a glance at a favorite piece can fill you with pride and a sense of accomplishment—which explains why tole painting is fast becoming one of the most popular creative hobbies in America!

Index